THE MEANING OF CONVERSION IN BUDDHISM

Also by Sangharakshita

A Survey of Buddhism
Flame in Darkness
The Enchanted Heart
The Three Jewels
Crossing the Stream
The Essence of Zen
The Thousand-Petalled Lotus
Human Enlightenment
The Religion of Art
The Ten Pillars of Buddhism
The Eternal Legacy
Travel Letters
Alternative Traditions
Conquering New Worlds
Ambedkar and Buddhism
The History of My Going for Refuge
The Taste of Freedom
New Currents in Western Buddhism
A Guide to the Buddhist Path
Learning to Walk
Vision and Transformation
The Buddha's Victory
Facing Mount Kanchenjunga
The FWBO and 'Protestant Buddhism'
The Drama of Cosmic Enlightenment
Wisdom Beyond Words
The Priceless Jewel
Who is the Buddha?

The Meaning of Orthodoxy in Buddhism
Mind Reactive and Creative
Going For Refuge
The Caves of Bhaja
My Relation to the Order
Hercules and the Birds and Other Poems
Buddhism and the West
Forty-Three Years Ago

SANGHARAKSHITA

THE MEANING OF CONVERSION
IN BUDDHISM

WINDHORSE PUBLICATIONS

Published by Windhorse Publications
Unit 1-316 The Custard Factory, Gibb Street, Birmingham, B9 4AA

Printed by The Cromwell Press,
Melksham, Wiltshire.

The cover shows a detail from the
Wheel of Life, Tibet, 19th century,
courtesy of the Ashmolean Museum, Oxford.

Cover design: Dhammarati

Illustration on page 33 by Aloka

British Library Cataloguing in Publication Data:
A catalogue record for this book is available from the British Library.

ISBN 0 904766 67 5

Contents

Editors' Preface

HOW IS ONE 'CONVERTED' TO BUDDHISM? In the old days, if you'd been in the right place at the right time, you might have come across the Buddha himself, wandering along a road in India, and a brief conversation with him might have been enough to convince you of the truth of his teaching. But in the West, at the end of the twentieth century, it's going to be rather different. Perhaps you get a book out of the library. Perhaps a friend tells you about some Buddhist teaching they have come across, or you get talking to someone on a train. Perhaps, in search of peace of mind, you go along to a Buddhist centre to learn meditation. Or perhaps you see a television documentary.

However you become aware of Buddhist ideas, somehow they make sense to you. You may feel that you've been a Buddhist all along without knowing it. You may even start calling yourself a Buddhist. But what does 'being a Buddhist' really mean? The ideal of Buddhism may be Enlightenment, but how do you set about becoming Enlightened? Presumably it isn't enough to give intellectual assent to, or even 'believe in', the ideas you've come across. What effect is Buddhism going to have on your own life?

What is it going to give you—and what is it going to demand of you?

These questions were perhaps uppermost in the minds of some of those who came to the Hampstead Buddhist Vihara on Sunday afternoons in 1966 to hear the venerable Sangharakshita speak on the theme of Buddhist conversion. At that time interest in Buddhism was growing in England, but that interest was for the most part intellectual. Books were being published, Buddhist groups were meeting, but the idea that Buddhism was not of merely scholarly interest but could have—was meant to have—a radical effect on one's whole way of life had not yet taken root.

It was this over-intellectual approach that Sangharakshita sought to challenge in the talks on which this book is based. He was himself well aware of the demands of the Buddhist life, having spent twenty years practising and teaching Buddhism in India before his return to England in 1964. Now he was addressing an audience consisting mostly of people for whom Buddhism was little more than an idea, albeit a very good one. Some of them, perhaps, were content to take a more or less academic interest, but many of them must have felt frustrated. They were attracted to Buddhism, but were unsure what this meant in practice. What did they do now?

Plunging into the heart of this question, Sangharakshita set about explaining the true meaning of conversion in Buddhism. He emphasized the need to commit oneself wholeheartedly to the Buddha's teaching, allowing it to change one's whole way of life. Being a Buddhist is a full-time occupation, not a hobby or an intellectual pastime; it is something to be taken seriously. And when you take something seriously, all sorts of practical questions arise. It's easy enough to talk about the importance of commitment, but how do you commit yourself? In each of the talks Sangharakshita took a pragmatic approach, on the basis that whilst it is important to know the theory, it is even more important to understand how to put it into practice.

He saw that if Buddhism was to be established in Britain it must be firmly based on the fundamental principles, the essentials of the Buddha's teachings, rather than on the style in which Buddhism was practised in other cultures, however attractive and exotic that style might be. He based his talks, therefore, on four traditional Buddhist teachings. The subjects he addressed in his first two talks—going for refuge to the Three Jewels and 'Entering the Stream'—have their origin in the Pali Canon, a collection of some of the earliest teachings of Buddhism. The subject-matter of the third talk, the arising of the will to Enlightenment, is a concept that lies at the very heart of Mahāyāna Buddhism, the second great phase of Buddhism in India. And the topic covered in the last talk, the 'turning about in the deepest seat of consciousness', derives also from the Mahāyāna, from the *Laṅkāvatāra Sūtra*.

No doubt these talks helped to convince many of those present in the audiences that if their conversion to Buddhism was to mean anything, they had to commit themselves to it wholeheartedly. Indeed, amongst them were several of those who would form the nucleus of the Friends of the Western Buddhist Order, which Sangharakshita founded the following year. *The Meaning of Conversion of Buddhism* has also proved to be a seminal work in terms of Sangharakshita's subsequent thought and teaching. Here, for example, we find his assertion of the primary importance of Going for Refuge. From this starting point was developed his teaching of the levels of Going for Refuge—provisional, effective, real, and absolute—the understanding of which has been crucial to the development of the Western Buddhist Order.

In considering the Sangha refuge, the reliance on the spiritual community, Sangharakshita has—over the years since these talks were given—further underlined the emphasis he then gave to the value of what he terms 'horizontal friendship'. Whilst communication between spiritual teacher and pupil is certainly important, there can be a tendency to think that this kind of 'vertical' relationship is the only spiritual friendship that matters. On the contrary, however, as Sangharakshita has pointed out, friendships with our peers in the spiritual life are crucial to our development.

Developing his appreciation of the importance of the arising of the bodhicitta, Sangharakshita gave a series of eight lectures devoted to a detailed exploration of the Bodhisattva Ideal, which greatly enlarged on the thinking outlined in Chapter Three of this book. In a lecture entitled 'The Awakening of the Bodhi Heart', for example, it was made clear that the arising of the bodhicitta cannot really be thought of as an individual experience, because it transcends individuality. The will to Enlightenment is therefore most likely to arise in a 'collective' situation, a situation in which the spiritual community is working together in harmony.

In this book, the four aspects of conversion discussed are presented in terms of progressively deepening spiritual development. Whilst this is a perfectly valid way of seeing them, Sangharakshita came to realize that these aspects of conversion can also be seen as different facets of the same experience. He saw Stream Entry, for example, as being equivalent to what he termed 'real' Going for Refuge, and he characterized the arising of the will to Enlightenment as the 'altruistic dimension' of Going for Refuge. Sangharakshita drew attention to these correlations in a talk given in Bombay in 1981, in which he related them also to other turning points in one's spiritual career, the going forth and the opening of the Dharma eye. Whilst we have not had room to add all Sangharakshita's expansions of these teachings to his original exposition of them nearly thirty years ago, the text has been augmented here and there with points from other lectures and seminars.

These days there is perhaps more awareness than there was in 1966 that Buddhism is a path to be followed, not just a teaching to be admired. But with the rich array of different forms of Buddhism now available to the fast growing number of Buddhist converts, and with the amount of media attention given to all kinds of spiritual philosophy, there is perhaps an even greater need for a clear understanding of what conversion in Buddhism might mean. So many people in the public eye are calling themselves Buddhists that to be converted to Buddhism seems almost fashionable. And even if one's interest in Buddhism is wholehearted, one may be confused about what being a Buddhist might really mean—especially when Buddhist ideas get mixed up with the latest psychological theories and techniques. Being a Buddhist requires effort of a kind which makes it only too tempting to settle down in a purely intellectual understanding of the spiritual life. For all these reasons a clear statement of the meaning of conversion in Buddhism, based on purely traditional Buddhist principles, and signalling the importance of commitment to the Buddhist life, is badly needed. This book is such a statement.

Jenny Wilks, Jinananda, and Vidyadevi
Spoken Word Project
February 1994

INTRODUCTION

WHAT IS CONVERSION? For many of us in the West, the word immediately conjures up the image of a missionary going forth armed with a Bible and a bottle of medicine to convert the heathen in the depths of some Eastern jungle. This is, of course, very much a stereotype, although one does come across rather alarming examples of it from time to time. I remember that when I was living in the Himalayan town of Kalimpong some forty years ago, someone showed me a copy of a Christmas card which was being sent out by a four-year-old girl, the daughter of a couple of missionaries who lived in Ghoom. This remarkable child was asking her little friends back in England to pray for the conversion of the 'heathen'—the heathen being, of course, all the Buddhists and Hindus in Ghoom and the surrounding area. In particular she asked the recipients of her cards to pray to Jesus that these heathens should stop doing their pujas. And for the benefit of those who might have been unfamiliar with this term for devotional practice, she added (in brackets) 'devil worship'.

This is obviously a very primitive conception of conversion; to be fair, Christian conversion is often misunderstood. It may popularly be thought to be the turning of the heathen from their heathenish ways to the light of the 'true faith' but it also has a much higher and more valuable meaning. The general meaning of the word conversion is clear enough; any dictionary will tell us that it means simply 'turning around'. And when one turns around, this involves a double movement: a movement away from something and also a movement towards something. So what is one turning away from, and what is one turning towards? For many people, both Christians and adherents of other faiths, 'conversion' means a turning from a lower to a higher way of life, from a worldly to a spiritual life. Conversion in this sense is often spoken of as a change of heart—a change of heart which leads you to stop running after the transitory things of this world and direct your attention and energy to the sublime, everlasting things of the spirit.

Put in this way, conversion is common to all religions in one form or another. The classic case is that of St Paul on the road to Damascus, but such sudden and dramatic conversions also occur in the Buddhist scriptures. One of the most notable examples is the case of the robber Angulimala, who changed in the course of a few days, perhaps even a few hours, into an emancipated being, if not an Enlightened one.* Indeed, conversion can happen even faster than that, according to an epitaph written in the sixteenth century by William Camden 'for a man killed by falling from his horse'. The epitaph goes:

Betwixt the stirrup and the ground
Mercy I asked, mercy I found.

---

* This story can be found in *The Collection of the Middle Length Sayings* (*Majjhima-nikaya*), vol.II, no.86, trans. I.B. Horner, Pali Text Society, London 1959.

This would suggest that, even for someone whose friends might have thought him spiritually speaking a no-hoper, conversion can come at the very last minute—'betwixt the stirrup and the ground'. More conventionally, of course, it occurs as what we call a 'death-bed conversion'. But while some people have these apparently genuinely instantaneous experiences, conversion can come about in a much more gradual way. There may be a 'moment of conversion', the experience may be sudden, even catastrophic, but then it dawns on you that actually your whole life, your whole being, has been building up to that moment over many years.

But however it comes to us, over a period of years or in a matter of seconds, the experience of conversion is of the greatest possible importance, because it marks the beginning of our spiritual life. The meaning of conversion therefore deserves our closest attention. However, although there have been many studies of the nature of conversion in Christianity,* there has as far as I know been no systematic study of Buddhist conversion. Perhaps, indeed, one might consider the meaning of conversion in Buddhism to be a simple matter, hardly worth studying. People tend to think: 'Once upon a time I was a Christian. Then I read a book about Buddhism, and I changed my faith. Now I'm a Buddhist and that's that.' But it is not really that simple. If we look at what the phenomenon of conversion means in Buddhism, we find that it occurs on several different levels and presents several different aspects.

In this book, four of these aspects are explored: Going for Refuge (or the transition from the Wheel of Life to the Spiral Path), Stream Entry, the arising of the will to Enlightenment, and what the *Laṅkāvatāra Sūtra* calls the 'turning about' (the term is

---

* See, for example, William James, *The Varieties of Religious Experience*, Harvard University Press, Cambridge 1985.

parāvṛitti, which can be translated quite literally as 'conversion'). This list, which includes some of the most fundamental of Buddhist terms, is by no means exhaustive, but it is sufficient to illustrate, or at least throw some light upon, what conversion means, not just to the aspiring Buddhist but to practising Buddhists at all levels of spiritual attainment, right up to Buddhahood itself.

Chapter One

GOING FOR REFUGE

IN A SENSE, GOING FOR REFUGE is the simplest, almost the most elementary, aspect of conversion in Buddhism; but in a wider, more comprehensive sense, it includes and informs all the other types and levels of conversion. So first, what is Going for Refuge? Although the term is so widely used in Buddhism, it can be rather mystifying when you first come across it. What does one mean by 'Refuge'? And who or what does one 'go for Refuge' to? The short answer is that as a practising Buddhist one goes for Refuge to the Buddha, the Enlightened teacher, to the Dharma, or his teaching of the way or path leading to Enlightenment, and to the Sangha, the community or Order of those progressing along that path in the direction of Enlightenment. These three Refuges are also commonly known as the Three Jewels.

In many traditional Buddhist cultures, Going for Refuge has become—it has to be said—little more than a formality. Just as if you want to be formally admitted into a Christian church you have to undergo the rite of baptism, in the same way, if you wish formally to signalize the fact that you consider yourself to be a Buddhist, you receive the Refuges and Precepts from an accredited representative of the Buddhist tradition, a bhikshu, and by doing this you formally join the Buddhist community. Some people therefore consider that Going for Refuge is just a matter of recitation. By saying 'To the Buddha for Refuge I go, to the Dharma for Refuge I go, to the Sangha for Refuge I go,' in Pali or Sanskrit, and repeating it three times, one is considered to have gone for Refuge. Sometimes people even speak of 'taking Refuge', although the Pali word *gacchāmi* means 'I go', not 'I take'. In many parts of the Buddhist world, Going for Refuge is understood in no deeper sense than this verbal repetition of a formula. People go along to the temple, or to a Buddhist meeting, recite these sentences, then go home and forget all about it. So far as they are concerned, they have gone for Refuge, conversion has taken place. They see no need to ponder the meaning deeply or try to explore its significance, much less still put it into practice.

This degeneration of Going for Refuge into a formality is a very unfortunate development. Nothing in the Buddha's teaching is meant to be practised mechanically or as a matter of mere tradition, without an understanding of its inner meaning and its relevance to one's own life. It behoves us, therefore, to take a closer look at the phrase 'Going for Refuge' and try to see what its significance really is. To begin with, what is meant by 'Refuge'? Refuge from what? The traditional explanations are quite clear on this point: the Three Jewels are a refuge from suffering. It is the existence of the Buddha, the Dharma, and the Sangha that makes it possible for us to escape from the unsatis-factoriness, the transitoriness, the conditionedness, the 'unreality' of the world as we experience it. In a well-known passage in the *Udāna*, one of the earliest Buddhist scriptures, the Buddha tells the monks that there exists an unborn, unmade, unoriginated, uncompounded Reality, and that it is this which makes it possible to escape from the born, the made, the put-together—in other words, from the world as we experience it.*

The Buddha, the Dharma, and the Sangha are called the Three Jewels because they represent the world of the highest spiritual values. Just as in the ordinary world jewels are the most precious of all material things, so in the spiritual world—in fact in the whole of existence—the Buddha, Dharma, and Sangha are those values which are the most sought after, which are ultimately the most desired and the most worthwhile, and from which all other values derive by way of direct or indirect reflection. When we call the Buddha, Dharma, and Sangha the Three Jewels, we are considering them in the abstract, as it were. We are considering their value—their ultimate or supreme value—as compared with all other things. When we speak of them as the Three Refuges, however, we are considering the practical implications of that evaluation. The fact that those values exist gives us the possibility of development, evolution, and progress far beyond our present comparatively low level. Considered as refuges, the Three Jewels represent the possibility of complete liberation from suffering.

It is no linguistic accident that we speak of *Going* for Refuge. You don't just *accept* the Three Refuges; you *go* for Refuge. This action is a total, unqualified reorientation of your life, your existence, your striving, in the direction of the Three Jewels or Refuges. When you say 'I go for Refuge' you are not only acknowledging that the Three Jewels are the most supremely valuable things in existence; you are also acting upon that acknowledgement. You see that the Three Jewels provide a possibility of escape into a higher spiritual dimension, and so you

---

* See *The Udana—Inspired Utterances of the Buddha*, 8.3, trans. John D. Ireland, Buddhist Publication Society, Kandy, Sri Lanka 1990.

go—you completely redirect and reorganize your life in the light of that realization. Bearing in mind the definition 'turning around', if this is not conversion it would be difficult to say what is.

It is all very well, of course, to say: 'Reorganize your life around the Three Jewels'; obviously this is something which is not easily done. We need to explore how it works out in concrete terms, and this we can do by looking at each of the Three Refuges in turn.

In practice, Going for Refuge to the Buddha means taking the Buddha (the historical Buddha Śākyamuni) as the living embodiment of the highest conceivable spiritual ideal. It means that after surveying and comparing all the great spiritual teachers, while fully appreciating each and every one of them, you nevertheless come to the conclusion that all their spiritual values and attainments are, as it were, summed up in the person of the Buddha. To your knowledge there is no attainment higher than his. If you regard any other being, any other teacher, as having gained a spiritual level or knowledge higher than that of the Buddha, then there is no Buddha Refuge for you. You may be an admirer of the Buddha, but you are not a Buddhist unless you see in the Buddha the highest embodiment of the highest spiritual ideal.

One might object, especially if one was universalistically inclined, that this is a rather narrow attitude. Why does one need to consider the Buddha to be supreme? Why not regard all great spiritual teachers as equal and have the same appreciation for them all—even go for refuge to them all? In fact, the Buddhist attitude is not narrow so much as pragmatic. We are concerned here not with matters of abstract theory, but with authentic, heartfelt, living spiritual practice. And in the spiritual life one of the most important elements, if not in a sense *the* most important element, is devotion. It is devotion which provides the driving power. The intellect, we might say, is like a motor car: the machinery is all there, but without the fuel, without the igniting spark, it just won't move. We may know all the philosophies and systems of religion, we may even be able to write and speak about them, but if our knowledge is just cold, intellectual, and abstract, if that living spark of inspiration, devotion, and faith is not there, we shall never make any progress.

Devotion flows most easily towards a person, or at least towards a personified embodiment of the ideal we want to reach. Because it is directed in this way, it is by its very nature exclusive. We cannot be deeply devoted to a number of spiritual ideals simultaneously. If we are going to develop devotion to an intensity which is capable of propelling us along the spiritual path in the direction of the goal, it must be fixed on just one figure, the one which we consider to be the highest. The Sanskrit term for faith or devotion, śraddhā, comes from a root which means 'to place the heart'; devotion is necessarily to some degree exclusive because the heart can truly be placed only on one object.

At the same time, intolerance has no place in Buddhism. In regarding the Buddha as pre-eminent, as the supremely Enlightened One above all other religious teachers, Buddhism does not dismiss, much less still condemn, any other religious teacher. Indeed, whilst Buddhists honestly and straightforwardly regard the Buddha as the greatest of all spiritual teachers that have ever lived, they are at the same time quite prepared to respect and even admire other spiritual leaders. Many Chinese Buddhists, for instance, entertain deep admiration and respect for Confucius and Lao Tsu. It is one of the great beauties of Buddhism that while Buddhists have a faith which is exclusive in the sense of being concentrated—they direct their whole heart's devotion to the Buddha—this faith is not exclusive in the sense of being intolerant or fanatical.

The word *dharma* has many meanings; as the second Refuge, the Dharma, it has two principal ones. Firstly it refers to the teaching of the Buddha, the Buddhavacana or word of the

Buddha; secondly it means the spiritual Law, Truth, or Ultimate Reality. These two meanings are obviously interconnected. The Buddha had a certain spiritual experience of Reality, and out of that experience he gave his teachings; so the formulated Dharma is the external expression, in terms of human thought, conceptions, and speech, of the Buddha's experience of the Dharma as Ultimate Reality.

On the intellectual plane, Going for Refuge to the Dharma means being convinced of the essential truth of the Buddha's teaching. One must be convinced that it exhibits clearly and unambiguously, above all other teachings, the way leading to Enlightenment. Obviously Going for Refuge to the Dharma in this sense involves knowledge of it, and in order to know the Dharma you have to study it. This, I am afraid, is where many of us fall down. However many Buddhist lectures we attend, however many books we read, if we cannot answer a simple factual question about the Four Noble Truths or the Eightfold Path or the twelve *nidānas*, what has been the point? Without any lasting knowledge of the Dharma, we can hardly be said to be Going for Refuge to it.

I once attended a talk by Krishnamurti in Bombay. It was a beautiful talk, absolutely crystal clear; but at the end a woman got up, almost tearing her hair out in frustration, and said in a voice quivering with emotion (as people's voices tended to in Krishnamurti's meetings): 'Sir, we have been following you and listening to you for forty years, but we do not seem to have got anywhere.' If as Buddhists we have not got anywhere, at least on the intellectual level, after forty years, or even after four years, even four months, it may well be because we have not got down to the study of Buddhism. If we were taking up engineering or medicine, or even pig-keeping, we would expect to have to study it; similarly, knowledge of Buddhism does not just come automatically when we say *'dhammaṁ saraṇaṁ gacchāmi'* ('To the

Dharma for Refuge I go'). Even the most devout Buddhist cannot bypass an intellectual acquaintance with the Buddha's teaching.

In one of his essays T.S. Eliot makes a caustic little remark which goes right to the point: 'People talk of transcending the intellect, but of course first one must have an intellect.' While we have to go beyond an intellectual understanding of the Dharma, we cannot afford to look down upon that understanding until we possess it. It is no good being 'deep and mystical', and thinking that we can skip the hard intellectual study of Buddhism. Study has its limitations, of course—we have to bear in mind that we are studying the expression of spiritual truths which ultimately have to be realized—but it is important to know the basic doctrinal principles thoroughly and be convinced of their truth. So in order to go for Refuge to the Dharma, you have to read books about it, talk about it, hear lectures about it, and develop a clear intellectual understanding of it—without in the end being confined or limited by that understanding.

This clear understanding is necessary but not, of course, sufficient. Going for Refuge to the Dharma means not just understanding the doctrines but realizing for oneself the principle or Reality which the doctrinal formulations represent. To put it more simply, Going for Refuge to the Dharma means the actual practice of the Dharma, through observance of Buddhist ethics, through meditation, and through the cultivation of transcendental Wisdom.

Just as Going for Refuge to the Buddha does not preclude intelligent receptivity to teachers from other traditions, so Going for Refuge to the Dharma need not exclude appreciation of other spiritual teachings, whether Hindu, Christian, Taoist, Confucian or whatever. Indeed, after leaving behind some other religion and penetrating deeply into Buddhism, we may be surprised to discover that we now understand our former religion better. As we begin to make sense of Buddhism we begin to find that all the other religions also make sense. The Buddhist would say that this is because the part cannot really be understood apart from the whole. Buddhism, as well as being a sublime and noble teaching, is comprehensive, neither rejecting nor repudiating any truth however humble, any spiritual discovery wheresoever made, but weaving them all into one great system, as it were, in which they all find the appropriate place. It is not, of course, that Buddhists take all other religions on their own valuation—if they did that they could not be Buddhists—but from a Buddhist perspective many teachings make sense at a level even deeper than their own estimation, and what is imperfect in them finds its fulfilment, its culmination, in the Buddha's teaching.

While having this comprehensive approach, however, Buddhism is not simply prepared to embrace all so-called religious teachings willy-nilly, and there are many teachings which it explicitly rejects. For instance, as far as Buddhism is concerned, the idea of a supreme being, a personal God who created the universe, is a wrong view which hinders the attainment of Enlightenment. A belief in God may be widely believed to be practically synonymous with religious faith, but it completely contradicts Buddhism's vision of Reality. If one accepts a doctrine which Buddhism regards as untrue then obviously one is no longer Going for Refuge to the Dharma. Here, as elsewhere, Buddhism follows a middle path, neither indiscriminately accepting all the teachings of other faiths, nor rejecting them wholesale. Like the pioneer in search of gold, Buddhism sifts and sorts out, rotating the pan so that all the dirt and water falls out, to reveal whatever grains of shining gold are there.

In all the cultures to which Buddhism has spread it has never totally rejected the existing religious traditions, but at the same time it has always gone beyond them, and jettisoned elements in those traditions which are incompatible with its own vision. That is why we find Buddhism having a purifying and refining influence on Hinduism in India, on Taoism in China, and on Shinto in Japan. Even in the West there are many Christians whose conception of Christianity has been elevated by their acquaintance with Buddhism, even though they have not chosen actually to become Buddhists.

In the West we tend to put up barricades and station ourselves either on one side or the other, as if to say 'Either take a religion or leave it. Either you are of it or you are not of it.' But Buddhism does not see things quite like that. It is more objective, more balanced. It does not hesitate to discard doctrines it considers to be immature, false, or untrue, even if they are sanctified by the name of religion. A teaching may be time-honoured, it may have been believed by millions of people for thousands of years, but this does not matter. If it is untrue, Buddhism rejects it. At the same time, if there is Reality, if there is beauty, in any other tradition, Buddhism is ready, willing, and even eager to accept and make use of it. This is what we find it doing in all ages and in all countries, and there is every reason to hope that the same process will continue in the West.

In the context of Going for Refuge, the third Jewel, the Sangha, is to be understood in three principal ways. Firstly, it means the transcendental hierarchy of Enlightened and partly-Enlightened persons existing on a purely spiritual plane. Things get rather complicated here, because this is not to say that these beings do not exist simultaneously here on earth. They are not necessarily organized into one spiritual community on a worldly level, however, because the unity of these beings is on a transcendental level. In Buddhist terminology, they are the Buddhas, Arhats, Bodhisattvas, and other great Enlightened and partly-Enlightened beings who have reached a level far above that of ordinary mundane life and consciousness. Secondly, Sangha means all those who have been ordained as Buddhists—traditionally this refers to the monastic Order of bhikshus or monks and of bhikshunīs or nuns. And thirdly, there is the *Mahāsaṅgha*. *Mahā* is Sanskrit for 'great', so this is the whole Buddhist community—all those who, to whatever degree, go for Refuge to the Three Jewels.*

We can go for Refuge to the Sangha in all these three senses. We go for Refuge to the Sangha as the spiritual or transcendental hierarchy when by our own spiritual attainments we become members of that hierarchy. We go for Refuge to the Sangha in the second sense either by being ordained into a Buddhist order or by supporting the order and relying on its members for spiritual advice and instruction. And we go for Refuge to the Mahā-saṅgha, the whole Buddhist community, simply by our fellowship with that community on whatever level, even simply on the ordinary social plane.**

Of course, the Sangha Refuge cannot really be understood in isolation from the context of the Three Jewels as a whole. Those who go for Refuge to the Sangha also necessarily go for Refuge to the Buddha and the Dharma. In other words, before you can effectively go for Refuge to the Sangha, you and all the people who form that Sangha need to have a common spiritual teacher or ideal and a common spiritual teaching or principle. It is this which makes it possible for people to come together into the spiritual community or Sangha. The fact that they go for Refuge to the Buddha and the Dharma naturally draws people together.

But is this all? What do we mean by 'together'? It does not mean just physical proximity. Coming together to sit in a kind of

---

* In the Western Buddhist Order, founded in 1968, ordination is neither monastic nor lay, but is based on effective Going for Refuge. This in a sense combines aspects of the second and third meanings of Sangha described here, and avoids the lay–monastic split which has been in many ways a hindrance to the spiritual vitality of Buddhism in the East.

** These three senses of the Sangha Refuge overlap to some extent with the different levels of Going for Refuge— provisional, effective, real, and absolute—outlined in Sangharakshita, *Going for Refuge*, Windhorse, Glasgow 1983.

congregation is not enough to form a Sangha. We may all quite sincerely take the Buddha for our spiritual teacher, and we may all be sincerely trying to practise, follow, and realize the Dharma. We may all agree on doctrinal questions, and even have the same meditation experiences. But these things do not in themselves mean that we constitute a Sangha. Going for Refuge to the Sangha is rather more subtle than that. It is essentially a matter of communication. When there is communication among those who go for Refuge to the Buddha and the Dharma, then there is Going for Refuge to the Sangha.

The communication which characterizes the Sangha is not merely an exchange of ideas and information. If I say to someone 'Last week I was in Norwich,' they will no doubt understand that statement perfectly—a successful exchange of ideas will have taken place—but there has not necessarily been any communication. If we find our contacts with others, even our friendships, frustrating and disappointing, if we find the exchanges we have with people at work or at parties a bit meaningless, it is because we are not using them as a medium for communication. So what is communication? It isn't very easy to say. For the purpose of exploring the Sangha Refuge, a working definition might be: 'a vital mutual responsiveness on the basis of a common ideal and a common principle'. This is communication in the context of Going for Refuge: a shared exploration of the spiritual world between people who are in a relationship of complete honesty and harmony. The communication is the exploration and the exploration is the communication; in this way spiritual progress takes place. It may not be clear exactly how it happens, but happen it certainly does.

The most common, or the most generally accepted, mode of this kind of communication is the relationship between spiritual teacher and disciple. When in this relationship there is a mutual responsiveness on the basis of a common allegiance to the Buddha and the Dharma, there is also a common refuge in the

Sangha. Such depth of communication is however not limited to that between teacher and disciple. It may also take place between those who are simply friends, or *kalyāṇa mitras*—'good friends' in the spiritual sense—to each other. Going for Refuge to the Sangha takes place when, on the basis of a common devotion to the Buddha and the Dharma, people explore together a spiritual dimension which neither could have explored on their own. Of course, beyond a certain point there is no question really of any sort of mutual relationship at all. In the process of communication and Going for Refuge to the Sangha, a dimension is eventually reached in which distinctions between the people involved no longer have any meaning—such distinctions have been transcended.

From all this we can begin to understand what Going for Refuge means, and in what sense it constitutes conversion. It is clearly not just a question of conversion from, say, Christianity to Buddhism, or of exchanging one set of ideas for another, even wrong ideas for right ones. It is infinitely more profound than that. Fundamentally it is a question of conversion from an ordinary mundane way of life to a spiritual, even a transcendental, way of life. More specifically, it consists of three distinct processes of turning around: firstly from limited ideals to an absolute, transcendental ideal; secondly from what Tennyson calls our 'little systems' that 'have their day' to a path based on unchanging spiritual principles and truths; and thirdly from meaningless worldly contact to meaningful communication. All these things are involved when we say: *Buddhaṁ saraṇaṁ gacchāmi, Dhammaṁ saraṇaṁ gacchāmi, Saṅghaṁ saraṇaṁ gacchāmi*—'To the Buddha for Refuge I go, to the Dharma for Refuge I go, to the Sangha for Refuge I go.'

Chapter Two

ENTERING THE STREAM

GOING FOR REFUGE MAY SEEM radical enough, involving as it does a total reorientation of our lives towards the spiritual values symbolized by the Three Jewels. This, however, is by no means all that is implied by conversion in Buddhism; indeed, it is only the beginning. We may start off by Going for Refuge to the Three Jewels, but in the end we must ourselves *become* the Three Jewels. There must be a permanent shift of the centre of gravity of our being from the conditioned to the Unconditioned, from saṁsāra to nirvāṇa. That is to say, conversion in Buddhism means not just a turning around *to* Buddhism, which happens when we go for Refuge to the Three Jewels, but a turning around *within* the context of our Buddhist practice itself.

I have chosen here to describe this essential shift in terms of gravity, but this particular point in one's spiritual career seems to lend itself to all kinds of metaphors. One of the most traditional, for example, is 'Stream Entry'. The 'stream' is the current which flows to Enlightenment, and the point of Stream Entry is the stage of spiritual practice at which your momentum towards Enlightenment is so strong that no obstacle can hinder your progress. Until this point, spiritual life is bound to be a struggle—you are going 'against the flow' of your own mundane nature—but when you enter the stream, all the struggling is over.

In this chapter, we shall be looking more closely at the crucial experience expressed by metaphors such as 'Stream Entry', a 'shift in gravity', and several more. But first we will focus on another aspect of conversion, one which comes earlier in the spiritual life, and which in fact corresponds to Going for Refuge to the Three Jewels. This experience can also be described in terms of a metaphor: the metaphor of the Wheel and the Spiral. And to understand the metaphor of the Wheel and the Spiral, to get just a glimmer of what it means, we have to go back two-thousand-five-hundred years to the foot of the Bodhi tree, back to the night of the Buddha's realization of supreme and perfect Enlightenment.

What was attained on that night, only a Buddha can say— indeed, not even a Buddha can really describe it. The *Laṅkāvatāra Sūtra* goes so far as to say that from the night of his Enlightenment to the night of his final passing away, the Buddha uttered not one word. In other words, the secret of his Enlightenment, the nature of the great transforming experience which he underwent, is incommunicable, and that is all that we can really say about it. We cannot say that it is this, or it is that, or even that it is not this or not that, because that would be to limit it. Nor can we say that it is this *and* that. According to the Buddha himself, we cannot even say that it is neither this nor that. All ways of speaking, all ways of telling, are transcended.

The Enlightenment experience is inexpressible, but we can get some hint of what it is by taking a more indirect view of it—by looking at it in terms of the difference which that experience made to the Buddha's outlook on existence as a whole. The scriptures tell us that when the Buddha surveyed the universe in the light of his supreme spiritual experience, he saw one prevailing principle or truth at work. He saw that the whole vast range and sweep of existence, from the lowest to the highest, in all its depth and breadth, was subject to what he subsequently called the law of conditionality. He saw that whatever arises anywhere in the universe, from the grossest material level up to the most subtle spiritual level, arises in dependence on conditions, and that when those conditions cease, the arisen phenomena also cease. He further saw that there are no exceptions to this principle. All things whatsoever within the sphere of phenomenal existence, from tiny cells to empires and great galactic systems, even feelings and thoughts, are governed by this law of conditionality. Expressed in conceptual terms, this great truth or law of 'conditioned co-production' (*pratītya-samut-pāda* in Sanskrit) became the basis of Buddhist thought.

There is a lot that could be said about conditionality, but there is one point in particular which we must understand, not only to enable us to grasp Buddhist thought but, even more importantly, to enable us to practise Buddhism effectively. This crucial fact is that conditionality is of two kinds: the 'cyclical' and the 'progressive' or 'spiral'.

In the cyclical mode of conditionality, there is a process of action and reaction between pairs of opposites: pleasure and pain, virtue and vice, birth and death and rebirth. What usually happens is that we swing back and forth between these pairs of opposites. We experience pleasure, for example, but sooner or later the pleasure goes and we experience pain; then, after some time, the pain swings back again into pleasure. In the spiral mode of conditionality, on the other hand, the succeeding factor increases the effect of the preceding one rather than negating it. When you are experiencing pleasure, instead of reacting in the cyclical order—with pain—you go from pleasure to happiness, and then from happiness to joy, from joy to rapture, and so on. The cyclical mode of conditionality, in which you go round and round, governs the saṃsāra, the round of conditioned existence, but the spiral mode, in which you go up and up, governs the spiritual life, especially as embodied in the path or way laid down by the Buddha, and the goal of that path, Enlightenment.

In the Tibetan Buddhist tradition, the round of conditioned or mundane existence is commonly represented in pictorial form. If you walked into a Tibetan temple or monastery you would see on the right-hand side of the entrance, inside the vestibule, an enormous painting of the Wheel of Life. In the hub of the Wheel, you would see three animals: a pig, a cock, and a snake, each biting the tail of the one in front. These symbolize the three basic human passions. The pig represents ignorance, in the sense of basic spiritual confusion, lack of an appreciation of spiritual values, and mental bewilderment of the deepest and darkest kind; the snake stands for anger, aversion, or irritation; and the cock symbolizes desire, craving, and lust in all their forms. These three animals are at the centre of the Wheel to indicate that it is our basic spiritual ignorance, together with the craving and aversion connected with it, that keeps us within the round of existence, undergoing birth and death and rebirth. The animals are depicted biting each other's tails because ignorance, craving, and hatred are all interconnected. If you have one, then you will have the other two. They cannot be separated, being different manifestations of the same primordial alienation from Reality.

Round the hub of the Wheel of Life you would see another circle, divided into two segments, one side black and the other white. In the white half there are people moving upwards, happy and smiling; in the black half people are tumbling down in a very wretched and terrible condition. The white side represents the path of virtue; the dark one the path of vice. So this circle represents, on one hand, the possibility of attaining to higher states within the round of existence, and on the other, the possibility of sinking to lower ones. The white and black paths do not refer to spiritual progress—or lack of it—towards the Unconditioned, but only to higher or lower levels of being (determined

The Tibetan Wheel of Life

by ethical or unethical actions) within conditioned existence itself.

Moving outwards from the hub, the third circle—which takes up the most space in the Wheel—is divided into six segments, each vividly depicting one of the spheres of sentient conditioned existence. At the top we see the world of the gods; next to that, working clockwise, the world of the *āsuras* or anti-gods; then the world of the hungry ghosts; then the lower realm of torment and suffering; above that, on the other side, that of the animals; and then the human world. These are the six spheres of sentient existence within which we may be reborn, according to whether the deeds we have performed and the thoughts we have entertained have been predominantly ethical or unethical.

So the meaning of the Wheel, as far as these three circles are concerned, is that sentient beings—and that means us—dominated by greed, anger, and ignorance, perform either skilful or unskilful actions and are reborn accordingly in an appropriate realm of conditioned existence. But there is also a fourth circle, right on the rim, divided into twelve segments; this represents the twelve *nidānas* or links of the chain of conditioned co-production, the chain which explains in detail how the whole process of life comes about. In the Wheel of Life's depiction of this chain, each segment contains an illustration of a particular *nidāna*, and these illustrations proceed clockwise round the Wheel.

At the top we see a blind man with a stick, an illustration of *avidyā*, which means ignorance in the spiritual sense of ignorance of the truth, ignorance of Reality. Next comes a potter with a wheel and pots, representing the *saṁskāras* or karma formations—volitional activities which issue from that ignorance. In other words, because of our primordial spiritual ignorance, and the things we have done in previous existences based on that ignorance, we have been reborn into our present life. Together, these two links make up what is called the 'cause process' of the past life, due to which we have arisen in this new existence.

The third image is a monkey climbing a flowering tree. This represents *vijñāna*, consciousness, which here means the first moment—almost, we might say, the first throb—of consciousness of the new being (or more accurately, the neither old nor new being) which arises in the womb of the mother at the time of conception. Fourth, arising in dependence on that, there is *nāma-rūpa*, the whole psychophysical organism (the image for this is a boat with four passengers, one of them steering). In dependence upon that arises *shaḍāyatana*, the six sense organs (in Buddhism, the mind is counted as a sixth sense) symbolized by a house with five windows and a door. Then, as the six sense organs come into contact with the external world, *sparśa,* touch or sensation, arises; the Wheel of Life's image for this is a man and woman embracing. And in dependence upon touch arises *vedanā* or feeling (pleasant, painful, or neutral), represented by a man with an arrow in his eye. This group of five *nidānas* together makes up the 'effect process' of the present life; they are the effects of actions based on ignorance performed in the previous life.

Next, there is a picture of a woman offering a drink to a man. This stands for the link of *tṛishṇā* or thirst—craving or desire in the widest sense. Then comes *upādāna*, clinging or attachment, represented by a man gathering fruit from a tree; then *bhāva* or becoming, the image for which is a pregnant woman. These three constitute the 'cause process' of the present life, because they set up actions which must bear fruit in the future, either in this life or in some future existence. Lastly *jāti* or birth and then *jarā-maraṇa*, old age and death, bring us full circle and constitute the 'effect process' of the future life. These last two cast imagery aside; the pictures simply show the truth in its starkness—a woman giving birth and a corpse being carried to the cremation ground.

So what does all this signify? It is a graphic illustration of the whole of human life. Due to our ignorance, and activities based on that ignorance, the seed of consciousness arises again in a new existence, which develops into a new psychophysical organism endowed with six senses. This inevitably comes into contact with the corresponding six sense-objects, as a result of which feelings and sensations arise. We start craving for the pleasant feelings and rejecting the unpleasant ones, while we remain indifferent to the neutral ones—and we therefore start clinging to what is pleasant and avoiding what is unpleasant. Habitually reacting in this way, grasping at pleasure and shrinking from pain, we eventually precipitate ourselves into another life, a life which is again subject to old age, disease, and death.

In this way, the twelve links explain how the whole process of life comes about. For explanatory purposes they are spread over three lives (past, present, and future), and in particular they show the alternation of cause and effect. First you get the cause process of the previous life; second, the effect process of the present life; third, the cause process of the present life; and fourth, the effect process of the future life. In this way there is an alternation between the two processes, cause and effect, a cyclical movement between pairs of opposites. This is all getting rather complicated, but it is leading us to a crucial point. Within the context of the three lives there are three points, known as the three *sandhis* or junctures, at which the cause process changes into the effect process or vice versa. *Sandhi* is an evocative term, being the Pali and Sanskrit word for dawn and twilight, the time when night passes over into day, or day into night.

The first *sandhi* occurs at the point where the volitional activities, the last link in the cause process of the past life, are followed by the arising of consciousness in the womb, the first link of the effect process of the present life. Another *sandhi* occurs at the juncture where in dependence upon feeling, the last link in the effect process of the present life, arises craving, the first link in the cause process of the present life. And the third juncture is where becoming, the last link in the cause process of the present life, gives rise to birth, the first link in the effect process of the future life.

The first and third of these *sandhis* are 'non-volitional'—that is, effect follows cause without our being able to do anything about it. But the second *sandhi*, between feeling and craving, is of crucial importance for us because it is a juncture at which we can make a choice. In fact, it is the point of intersection between the two kinds of conditionality, the cyclical and the progressive. This is where we either make a mess of things and as a result revolve once again in the Wheel, or start to progress and enter the Spiral. So we need to understand exactly what happens at this point.

All the time, whatever we are doing, even when we are just sitting reading a book, various sensations are impinging upon us—sensations of cold, heat, sound, light, and so on. All these sensations, whether we are aware of them or not, are either pleasant, painful, or neutral. Now, as these feelings arise, how do we react? To pleasant sensations we react most of the time with craving. We want them to continue, we don't want to lose them, so we try to cling on to them. Our natural tendency is to try to repeat pleasant experiences. This is the fatal mistake we are only too apt to make. We are not content to let the experience come and go; we want to perpetuate it, and so we react with craving. If, on the other hand, the sensation is unpleasant, painful, or at least unsatisfactory, we instinctively, even compulsively, try to thrust it away from us. We don't want it. We don't want anything to do with it. We try to escape from it. In short, we react with aversion. And if we feel a sensation which is neither pleasant nor painful, we just remain confused. Not knowing whether to grasp it or reject it, we react with bewilderment.

This is how we react all the time to the sensations and experiences that are continually impinging upon our consciousness through all the senses, including the mind. In this way an effect process is followed by a cause process, and we circle once more in the round of existence. The Wheel of Life makes one more revolution, and all the conditions are created or recreated for a fresh rebirth. This is where it all happens, at the point where in dependence upon feeling there arises craving.

But suppose we do not react in this way. Suppose, when sensations and feelings befall us, we do not react with craving or aversion or confusion. Suppose we can stop the process, suppose we can stop the Wheel turning—then what happens? Quite simply, what happens then is that mundane, conditioned existence comes to an end, and only the transcendental is left. We attain Enlightenment, nirvāṇa, or whatever else we like to call it.

The next question is how to stop the process. It is easy to say, but how do we do it? Broadly speaking, there are two ways of ensuring that feeling is not succeeded by craving, two ways of ensuring that the Wheel does not make another revolution. The first is a sudden way which shatters the Wheel at a single blow; the second is a gradual way which progressively slows the Wheel down, gently applying a brake to bring the whole thing slowly to a halt.

The sudden way may sound rather Zen-like, Zen being famous for its abrupt methods, but we can illustrate it with a story not from the Zen tradition but from the *Udāna* of the Pali Canon: the story of Bāhiya.* Bāhiya was a monk who had been admitted to the order in some distant part of the country, which meant that he had never had the chance to meet the Buddha or ask him any questions. He wanted to put this right as soon as possible, so he made the long journey to the place where the Buddha was staying. When he arrived, however, the Buddha was out on his daily alms round, going from house to house for food. Having come so far, Bāhiya wasn't going to hang around waiting for the

---

* *The Udana—Inspired Utterances of the Buddha*, 1.10, trans. John D. Ireland, Buddhist Publication Society, Kandy, Sri Lanka 1990.

Buddha to come back, so he asked someone which direction the Buddha had taken and eagerly went after him.

It wasn't long before he caught up with the Buddha, still walking mindfully from door to door. Bāhiya had no thought of waiting for a suitable moment to speak with his teacher for the first time. Almost treading on the Buddha's heels, he called out, no doubt rather breathlessly, 'Please give me a teaching.' But it was the Buddha's custom never to speak during his alms round, so he ignored Bāhiya's request and kept on walking. A second time Bāhiya asked, even more urgently this time, 'Please give me a teaching.' But again the Buddha ignored him and kept walking. Refusing to give up, Bāhiya made his request for a third time. And this time he got a response. It was apparently a rule with the Buddha that if anyone asked him something three times, he would answer the question, whatever it was and however serious the consequences might be for the questioner. So, stopping in his tracks, he turned round, gave Bāhiya a very direct look, and said, 'In the seen, only the seen. In the heard, only the heard. In the touched, only the touched. In the tasted, only the tasted. In the smelt, only the smelt. In the thought, only the thought.' He then turned round and went on with his alms round—and Bāhiya became Enlightened on the spot.

The Buddha was saying, in effect, 'Don't react.' If a sound impinges on your eardrums, it's just a sound—you don't have to react to it. You don't have to like it or dislike it. You don't have to want it to continue or want it to stop. 'In the heard, only the heard.' The same goes for the seen, the touched, the tasted, the smelt, and even the thought. Don't react. Let the bare experience be there, but don't make that experience the basis for any action or reaction in the cyclical order. If you can do that, you abruptly stop the Wheel revolving and realize nirvāṇa here and now, on the spot—as Bāhiya, it seems, actually did.

The sudden way is obviously very, very difficult. In fact, it may even sound impossible. The example of Bāhiya, and many similar cases, shows that it *is* possible, but for most people it is a much more reliable and sound procedure to try to follow not this sudden path but the gradual path (which of course does not mean the 'never-never path'!). The gradual path can be laid out in terms of the Noble Eightfold Path, the seven stages of purification, the ten *bhūmis*, and many other formulations, but in this context it is perhaps best explained in terms of the twelve positive links which constitute, psychologically and spiritually, the successive stages of the progressive movement of conditionality as it spirals away from the Wheel. For our present purposes we shall ignore the last four of these, as they take us beyond Stream Entry.* Here we shall be concerned only with the first eight links, and particularly with the first and second and with the seventh and eighth.

The first and second links leading up and away from the cyclical mode of action and reaction are *duḥkha*, suffering or unsatisfactoriness, and *śraddhā*, faith or confidence. In the twelve links of the Wheel of Life, suffering corresponds to feeling, the last link in the effect process of the present life, and faith corresponds to craving, the first link in the cause process of the present life. What this means is that when sensations and experiences impinge upon us we do not have to react with craving and thus perpetuate the cyclical movement of existence. We can react instead in a positive way. As we experience pleasant, unpleasant, and neutral feelings, we can begin to see, to feel, that none of them are really very satisfactory, not even the pleasant ones. Even they are not enough. Even if we could perpetuate pleasant experiences and eliminate painful ones, there would still be some hidden lack, something unsatisfied and frustrated.

---

* The twelve links of the Spiral Path are described in detail in Sangharakshita, *The Three Jewels*, Windhorse, Glasgow 1991, chap.13.

So we begin to see, we begin to feel, we begin to realize, that this whole conditioned existence—our life, our ordinary experience—is not enough. It cannot give us permanent, true satisfaction or happiness. If we analyse it deeply, in the long run it is unsatisfactory.

As we start to see that this is so, we begin to sit loose to mundane existence. We begin to detach ourselves from it. We don't care about it so much. We start thinking that there must be something higher, something beyond, something which can give satisfaction of a more permanent, deeper, and truer nature—in a word, something spiritual, even something transcendental. So we begin to shift the focus of our interest, and eventually we develop faith. We 'place the heart' less and less on our everyday experience, and more and more on the Unconditioned, the transcendental. At first our faith may be confused, vague, and inchoate, but gradually it clears, it settles down, it strengthens, and eventually it becomes faith or confidence in the Three Jewels. We begin to see the Buddha, the Dharma, and the Sangha as the embodiments of those higher spiritual values which both stand above and beyond the world yet at the same time give meaning and significance to the world. We place our heart more and more on them, and when that faith waxes strong enough we are galvanized into action and we go for Refuge.

In this way, faith is the positive, spiritual counterpart of craving. Instead of craving arising in dependence upon feeling, we find that faith in the Unconditioned (as represented by the Three Jewels) arises in dependence upon the experience of the unsatisfactoriness of conditioned existence. At this juncture we have left the Wheel and entered the Spiral; we have begun to move not in a cyclical order, but in a progressive, spiral order. We have, in fact, entered upon the path leading to nirvāṇa. This transition from the Wheel to the Spiral is a moment of conversion. In fact, although it is expressed in different terms, it corresponds to conversion in the sense of Going for Refuge, and there is the same

sense of movement—away from the endless round of conditioned existence, towards the infinite Spiral of the transcendental. The transition from the Wheel to the Spiral still leaves us
a long way short of Stream Entry, but we could say—mixing our
metaphors—that at this stage we begin to enter the tributary
which leads, by way of the next six positive progressive links of
the Spiral, to the Stream.

In dependence upon faith there arises *prāmodya*, usually translated as satisfaction or delight. This is the feeling which arises
when you see that you have no cause for self-reproach because
you have not done anything, so far as you can recollect, which
makes you feel guilty. You have a perfectly clear conscience. In
Buddhism, great importance is attached to this state. If you have
anything on your mind that you regret or are ashamed of,
anything unatoned for, anything you have not come to terms
with, it is difficult, if not impossible, to make any further
progress, certainly not progress in meditation. Buddhists therefore carry out various practices of confession of faults and self-
purification which eliminate remorse or guilt and replace it with
this state of satisfaction and delight, this state in which you are
on good terms with yourself.

It is important, of course, to distinguish clearly between
genuine remorse for unskilful actions of body, speech, and mind,
and the irrational sense of guilt which dogs so many people,
often because it has been instilled into them from early
childhood, whether through the pervasive Christian doctrine of
original sin or by some other means. In Buddhism, confession of
faults is a straightforward acknowledgement of whatever one
has done out of craving, hatred, or delusion. To be able to confess
in this way requires not an abject submission to some external
power but an awareness that one is responsible for one's own
actions and a confidence that one is capable of developing skilful
mental states. As the terms skilful and unskilful indicate, in the

Buddhist way of looking at things there is no question of ir-
redeemable evil.

On the basis of this mental state of delight there arises *prīti*,
which is usually translated as interest, enthusiasm, rapture, or
even ecstasy. It represents an upsurge of joy from your very
depths as a consequence of the liberation of all the emotional
energies which have previously been blocked up, in the form of
various mental conflicts, in the subconscious or even unconscious mind. Something lifts from your mind, freed energy
comes bubbling up from within, and you feel much lighter.
When all these submerged emotional energies are released, there
is an experience not only of release but also of intense joy,
enthusiasm, and rapture. It is psychophysical—an experience of
the body as well as of the mind—so that your hair may stand on
end and you may shed tears.

In dependence upon this experience of rapture, which can
reach a very great degree of intensity, there arises *praśrabdhi*—
repose or tranquillity. This represents the calming, the dying
away, of the purely bodily manifestations of *prīti*. And once *prīti*
has died away, what is left is a state of happiness, *sukha*, in which
there is no sense consciousness. *Sukha*, which arises in dependence upon *praśrabdhi*, is a purely mental—or rather spiritual—
feeling of bliss; this pervades the entire being with a
concentrating and integrating effect which harmonizes it and
makes it whole. Then, in dependence on this experience of bliss,
there arises a state called *samādhi*. The usual translation is
'concentration', but this is clearly far from adequate. *Samādhi* is
really an experience of perfect wholeness at a very high level of
awareness.

At this point—and we have come quite a long way—we need
to acknowledge two important facts. In the first place, *samādhi* is
not something which can be acquired forcibly or artificially by
means of exercises or techniques. They may be of incidental help,
but fundamentally *samādhi* represents a spiritual growth or

evolution of the whole being. It is not enough just to concentrate your mind on an object for half an hour at a time if the rest of your life is pulling in the opposite direction. If ninety-nine per cent of your life is oriented in the direction of the mundane, it is no use just spending half an hour a day trying to orient it in a spiritual direction. That would be like taking an elastic band and pulling it taut—as soon as you release it, it snaps back. Unfortunately, this is how meditation is most commonly practised. Meditation proper, however, represents the spearhead of a basic reorientation of one's whole being. Mere forcible fixation of the mind for a period of time on a certain point or object is certainly not true meditation in the sense of the total growth or spiritual evolution of the whole being.

The second fact is that it is possible for us to fall back from these first seven stages on the Spiral. Although they are part of the Spiral, although they do not constitute a cyclical reaction, although they are part of the path to nirvāṇa, regression from them is possible. Even when you have gone up to *samādhi*, you can descend into bliss. From that you can lapse into tranquillity, from that into rapture, from that down into faith—and in that way you re-enter the Wheel. And this, of course, is what usually happens. Even if we really succeed in getting up the Spiral so far, up all those seven stages, it is only for a while. Even if it is a real experience, a real development—even if we are not just pulling the elastic—the experience is only temporary and we still fall back. We can balance ourselves at that level for a few minutes, but then we sink down and down until we are once again going round the Wheel. This happens because this section of the Spiral, these seven stages from the experience of unsatisfactoriness up to *samādhi*, are still subject to what we could call the 'gravitational pull' of the round of existence, the Wheel of Life.

So what is the point of it all? Is there any more sense in the spiritual life than in the endless chore given to Sisyphus in Hades, of pushing a great stone up a mountainside just so that it can roll all the way down again? Or can we get so far up the Spiral that there is no possibility of regression? Is it possible to reach a vantage point from which there is no falling back to the Wheel, or are we bound to go up and down like a yo-yo for all eternity?

The eighth positive *nidāna* provides the way out of this dismal predicament. In dependence upon *samādhi* arises *yathābhūta-jñānadarśana*—'knowledge and vision of things as they really are'. In other words, in dependence upon the pure, concentrated, integrated, totally balanced mundane mind, at the highest pitch of its development, there arises transcendental wisdom. So how does this come about? What is really involved in this development?

Knowledge and vision of things as they really are arises when, in the state of *samādhi*, we get our first glimpse of Reality itself, free from all veils and obscurations. It's like the moment when you get up to the top of a high mountain and the clouds roll aside to reveal the vast expanse of the horizon. *Samādhi* represents getting to the peak, the vantage point from which you can see Reality itself.

But how, in practice, do we glimpse Reality? Does it just arise spontaneously, or can we consciously work towards the experience? Well, the answer is that both are possible. For some people, Insight does come quite spontaneously. We don't know why a vision of Reality is just 'given' to some people—perhaps the reasons are hidden within the depths of their past lives. But one need not wait around for the experience to arise spontaneously. It can be developed on the basis of *samādhi* or, to put it more accurately, the conditions for the possibility of its arising can be created. It is not that you do this, that, and the other, and then you get knowledge and vision of things as they are, like getting a bar of chocolate out of a slot machine. The arising of Insight is not within the sphere of causality at all. We are dealing, after all, with the Unconditioned.

According to the Buddhist tradition, we can induce this experience (without of course implying anything artificial or even causative by such an expression) through the contemplation, in a state of *samādhi*, of the three marks or characteristics (*lakshaṇas* in Sanskrit) of all conditioned things. These characteristics are that conditioned things are unsatisfactory, impermanent, and, in the depths of their being, devoid of self—devoid, that is, of any separate, unchanging individuality which might mark them off from all other things.

Another way of approaching this experience is to contemplate the idea of nirvāṇa. I say *idea* because we have not yet got nirvāṇa itself into view; but in the state of *samādhi* we can bring to mind the idea of nirvāṇa, in whatever way appeals to us. As we are doing this, a flash of Insight may illuminate what nirvāṇa *really* is, and at that instant we enter upon the transcendental path of vision, the *darśana mārga*; or, to bring in another of the metaphors which describe this moment, we enter the Stream.

Another way to put it, of course, is the one mentioned at the beginning of the chapter. At this point one's personal centre of gravity has permanently shifted from the conditioned to the Unconditioned, so that from now onwards one is not just oriented in the direction of nirvāṇa, but actually moving irrevocably towards it. From this point on progress is assured, because one has reached that part of the Spiral which is not subject to any gravitational pull from the mundane, from the Wheel of Life.

To develop the metaphor of gravity a little, we may say that one's progress is rather like that of a space probe launched from the Earth. After a certain distance—so many thousand miles—it is no longer so affected by the Earth's field of gravity and begins to be influenced instead by the gravitational pull of the Moon, Mars, or whichever body it is heading for. So at a certain point the gravitational pull of the Wheel of Life ceases to have an influence, and one begins to feel more and more powerfully and decisively the gravitational pull of the Unconditioned, of nirvāṇa. This is the moment of conversion *within* Buddhist practice, the beginning of the transformation from a conditioned to an Unconditioned mode of being. According to Buddhist tradition, if we reach up this far, if we undergo conversion in this sense, we are assured of Enlightenment within no more than seven further rebirths in the wheel of conditioned existence.

All this is to look at the experience subjectively—from within, as it were. It can be described more objectively as consisting in the bursting asunder of three fetters. This is, of course, to bring in another metaphor—and again it is a traditional one. The Pali Canon enumerates ten fetters which bind us to the Wheel of Life. When all ten have been broken, Enlightenment is attained; the Stream Entrant is said to have broken the first three of them. The first of these three fetters is *satkāya-dṛishṭi*, usually translated as 'self-view' (*satkāya* means 'personal' or 'individual', and *dṛishṭi* means 'view' or 'doctrine'). *Satkāya-dṛishṭi* is the view that 'I' constitute something ultimate; that I, as I know myself here and now, with this particular body and mind, this particular history, represent a sort of unchanging, fixed entity. In other words it is the belief that 'I' am real.

This 'fixed self-view' is the biggest mistake of all, according to Buddhism, and it is the first fetter to be broken; you cannot enter the Stream unless you overcome it. Indeed, *you* do not enter the Stream at all. The whole point is that you cannot enter the Stream until you have detached yourself from name and form, from personal existence, from all the things that you think of as being 'you'—in short, until you have realized that you are not ultimately real. This is not to say, of course, that there is no such thing as the 'self', though this is how the Buddhist doctrine of *anātman* (literally 'no-self') is often misunderstood. The point is that we do not have an *unchanging* self. There is nothing fixed, 'underneath it all', about us; every single aspect of our being is subject to change. We have an empirical reality, it could be said, but not an ultimate reality. So this fixed self-view is a tremendous fetter, and one which is not easily broken.

The second fetter is *vicikitsā*, which is usually translated as 'doubt', although it is not really so much doubt as doubtfulness. It is a sort of wavering or hesitation. You hear about the Buddha, you listen to his teachings, you meet people who are trying to put those teachings into practice, but you hesitate. You say: 'Yes, well, it sounds good, but…', 'I'd like to give it a try, but…', 'I have nothing against it, but…'. That 'but' which is always coming in indicates that you are bound by the fetter of doubt. You don't quite believe, but you don't quite disbelieve either; you are wavering and hesitating between the two, which is a horrible state to be in. Unfortunately it is also a very common state. So many people go along to Buddhist groups and hear a few lectures, or read a few books, but never actually do anything about it. *Vicikitsā* is this kind of refusal to commit oneself unreservedly to the spiritual life; you hear about it, talk about it, but you keep holding back. How can you become a Stream Entrant if you persist in dithering on the bank? If you want to swim, it is no use hesitating on the edge wondering how warm or cold or deep the water is—you just have to jump in. *Vicikitsā* is that fear of jumping in, that refusal to commit oneself, that viewing from a distance without participating.

The third fetter is *śīlavrata-parāmarśa*. This always used to be translated as 'dependence upon rites and ceremonies', a translation which has given rise to a great deal of misunderstanding. *Śīla* means a moral observance or precept, *vrata* means a religious practice or observance (an example given in the scriptures is the Brahminical practice of tending the sacred fire), and *parāmarśa* means attachment or clinging. This fetter therefore represents dependence upon moral rules and religious practices *as ends in themselves*. This does not mean that practices such as observing the Precepts and engaging in religious ceremonies are a fetter *in themselves*; such practices are of course very beneficial.

It only means that if we cling on to these practices, forgetting that they are only means to an end, they will become a fetter which holds us back and prevents us from entering the Stream.

Precepts and practices become fetters when you carry them out almost as if you were hypnotized, without thinking: 'What does this mean?' 'Where is this getting me?' 'Is this actually doing any good?' So this fetter is really—roughly speaking—about conventional morals and religion. Conventional attachment to morality and religion, though not bad in a way, doesn't get you very far along the spiritual path, and it can even prevent you from entering the Stream. You can meet people who seem very ethical and noble, who observe all the Precepts, but who are a bit obsessed with their own virtue, a bit 'holier than thou'. They make a whip of their own virtue—as the saying goes—with which to beat other people. It is not that we should discard such things as precepts and devotional practices; that would be to go to the opposite extreme, which would be even more damaging. We need to make full and exhaustive use of them, but always remembering that they serve a purpose that lies beyond them.

As long as these three fetters—belief in one's 'self' as ultimately real, refusal to commit oneself unreservedly to the spiritual life, and dependence on moral rules and religious practices as ends in themselves—remain unbroken, no Stream Entry is possible. No escape from the gravitational pull of the conditioned is possible. One is bound to fall back down the Spiral and continue circling round the Wheel of Life. In other words, only with the breaking of these fetters is real conversion within Buddhism possible—conversion, that is, in the sense of a permanent transition from the conditioned to the Unconditioned mode of awareness and being.

Chapter Three

THE ARISING OF THE BODHICITTA

HAVING LOOKED AT CONVERSION *TO* BUDDHISM, and conversion *within* Buddhism, one might think that it is hardly possible to go any further, and in a sense—though only in a sense—this is true. But conversion in Buddhism not only has different levels; it can also be approached from different aspects and points of view. This brings us to conversion understood in terms of what is known in Mahāyāna Buddhism as the *bodhicitta utpāda*.*

We can provisionally render this term *bodhicitta utpāda* as 'the arising (*utpāda*) of the will (*citta*) to Enlightenment (*bodhi*)', but the term *bodhi* in particular needs a little more elucidation. It derives from a Sanskrit root meaning 'to know' or 'to understand', so it comes to mean 'understanding', 'wisdom', or even 'Enlightenment'. Traditional Buddhism distinguishes three kinds of bodhi: *srāvaka-bodhi*, 'Enlightenment of the disciple'; *pratyeka-bodhi*, 'private' or 'individual' Enlightenment; and *anuttara-samyaksambodhi*, 'unsurpassed, perfect Enlightenment'.

---

* In the 1,500 years or so during which Buddhism flourished in India, it went through three great phases, each lasting about 500 years: the Hinayāna ('lesser way'), the Mahāyāna ('great way'), and the Vajrayāna ('diamond way').

Until we have grasped what is meant by these three kinds of Enlightenment, there is much in the development of the history of Buddhist thought, especially in India, which we are not really in a position to understand.

Srāvaka literally means 'one who hears'; it is the Indian word for a disciple. However, a disciple not only hears with the ear, but also hears within; that is, he or she is receptive to the word of the teacher. *Srāva-kabodhi*, the Enlightenment of the disciple or hearer, therefore means the illumination which is gained not only by one's own effort but also on the basis of having been taught the method and discipline by someone else. Having been shown the path, one makes an effort and gains Enlightenment. However, one makes no attempt to communicate that experience to anyone else; one has a teacher but no disciples.

Pratyeka-bodhi differs from *srāvaka-bodhi* in that it is gained without the benefit of a teacher's instruction; one discovers the path for oneself. This is, of course, very difficult to achieve, and it is therefore very rare. And having attained Enlightenment in this way, one makes no attempt to communicate one's knowledge and experience to anyone else: hence 'private' or 'individual' Enlightenment.

Thirdly, there is *anuttara-samyaksambodhi*: unsurpassed, perfect Enlightenment. This too is gained without a teacher, but having been gained it is not kept to oneself but communicated to other beings so that they may have the opportunity of sharing the experience of Enlightenment. Gaining Enlightenment 'without a teacher' is to be understood in quite a narrow sense, of course, because it refers only to the present existence. Having been shown the way by others in previous lives, one has accumulated sufficient momentum to be carried through the present existence without a teacher, and to make the ultimate discovery by oneself.

At this stage a very important question arises, a question with far-reaching implications. What is the real, basic difference between these three kinds of bodhi? Are we concerned here with three different types of spiritual experience, or is it one and the same Enlightenment in each case? Is the difference between these three kinds of bodhi essential or merely accidental? When we first come across them, we might naturally conclude that the difference is circumstantial, or even adventitious, but in fact it is much more fundamental than that. Provisionally, the three bodhis may be said to represent three grades of Enlightenment within a hierarchical structure, the third of which is the highest, the consummation as it were, of the whole series.

If we want to identify the single essential distinction between these 'grades', we can simplify things by amalgamating the first and second of them and setting them apart from the third, *anuttara-samyaksambodhi*. The basic difference between these two categories obviously lies in the relation of the Enlightened being to other, unenlightened, people. The first group, whether they gain Enlightenment with or without a teacher, do not communicate their experience, whereas the second group do. This difference between the two is neither accidental nor merely external, because the communication, the 'giving away', of spiritual experience is not at all the same as the giving of material things. If we happen to acquire a precious stone, the jewel itself remains the same whether we keep it or give it away. But with spiritual experiences it is not like that in the least, because something far more subtle, delicate, and complex is involved. A spiritual experience which can be kept to oneself, we can say, is not the same as one which is communicated—which indeed *has* to be communicated, in the sense that the very nature of the experience *demands* that it should be communicated.

The fundamental difference between these two kinds of spiritual experience lies in whether or not the experience includes a feeling of selfhood. The feeling of selfhood has various forms, some gross and easily detected, others infinitely subtle and extremely difficult to detect. The subtlest of all the forms of this feeling is the form which arises in connection with the gaining of Enlightenment itself. We have a certain experience which we take as tending in the direction of Enlightenment, but then we attach to that experience a feeling that this is *my* experience, *my* Enlightenment, this is what *I* have gained. It is because this subtle feeling of selfhood arises that we may consider it possible not to communicate our experience to others. From the mundane point of view it may be a very high and sublime experience, but it is not the experience of unsurpassed, perfect Enlightenment; it is not the Enlightenment of the Buddha himself. So long as that feeling of 'my' can be attached to it, it is not the ultimate experience.

When we speak of conversion in Buddhism in terms of the arising of the bodhicitta—the will to Enlightenment—it is the second of these two kinds of Enlightenment which is meant: the unsurpassed, perfect Enlightenment, Enlightenment for the benefit of all sentient beings. So the will to Enlightenment is the aspiration to that Enlightenment wherein there is not a shadow of selfhood and which, paradoxically, cannot therefore be called 'mine'. There is no question of keeping it to oneself; by definition, it *has* to be communicated.

Having arrived at a sense of the meaning of *bodhi*, we need to find out a bit more about *citta*. *Citta* is usually translated as 'thought', and therefore bodhicitta is often translated as 'the thought of Enlightenment' as though it were a concept or idea about Enlightenment. But this is exactly what it is not. It has nothing to do with thought in that discursive or abstract conceptual sense at all. *Citta* represents an immensely powerful drive, a drive which is not unconscious but perfectly aware, a drive which has one's whole being behind it. It is better, therefore, to speak not of the thought of Enlightenment but of the *will to* Enlightenment, although even this is not quite accurate because this 'will' is infinitely more powerful than determination in the ordinary sense.

Finally, *utpāda* literally means 'arising': hence our working translation of *bodhicitta-utpāda* as 'the arising of the will to Enlightenment'. The arising of the bodhicitta is the initial process of orienting all one's energies and all one's strength, at all levels of one's being and personality, in the direction of Enlightenment understood as unsurpassed, perfect Enlightenment, Enlightenment for the benefit and welfare of all sentient beings.

Having worked out an appropriate translation, we can now turn to consider what light the arising of the will to Enlightenment sheds on the meaning of conversion in Buddhism. It can be said to represent conversion from an individualistic conception of Enlightenment to a non-individualistic ideal of Enlightenment, from the kind of Enlightenment which can be kept to oneself to the kind of Enlightenment which cannot possibly be kept to oneself. In other words, it represents a transition, a breakthrough, from that last most subtle sense of spiritual selfhood to an experience of complete and total selflessness.

Obviously this aspect of conversion is very important indeed, but it is not so easy to put your finger on it and say 'It is like this' or 'It occurs at a certain point,' in the way that you can with Going for Refuge and Stream Entry. One might even say that this type of conversion can occur at any stage of spiritual development, or in connection with any spiritual experience. This is why in Mahāyāna Buddhism there is the practice of 'turning over'— that is to say, turning over one's merits to the cause of perfect Enlightenment. Although it is often neglected, this is one of the most important teachings in the whole of Buddhism. In the Perfection of Wisdom scriptures the Bodhisattva (the Mahāyāna's idea of the Buddhist *par excellence*) is advised: 'Whenever you perform any good action, whenever you practise morality, or meditate, or help anybody, or give anything, turn over the merit—dedicate it to the cause of perfect Enlightenment.' In other words, don't think: 'This skilful action is going to help *me* attain liberation.' Instead, reflect or resolve: 'Whatever merit derives from my good deeds, I dedicate it to Enlightenment not just for my own benefit but for the benefit of all.' By practising regularly and systematically in this way, we ensure that in the course of our spiritual lives we do not build up a subtle spiritual selfhood which would eventually rise up and bar our way to the ultimate spiritual attainment, unsurpassed perfect Enlightenment.

The Bodhisattva is further told that this transference of merit in the direction of Enlightenment for the benefit of all beings is possible only on the basis of some insight into the doctrine of *śūnyatā* (which is often translated 'voidness' but really means 'non-dual Reality'), according to which there is no substantial distinction between self and other. However, this practice of turning over the merits accruing from good deeds should accompany us all along the spiritual path; we need not—cannot—leave it until Insight arises. On the other hand, it is not something you do once and for all—nor is it the case that if you did it last week you can forget about it until next year. It is something you have to do all the time, as a constant accompaniment to every practice, throughout your spiritual life.

Actually, this is not the only way to guard against spiritual individualism. You can, if you so wish—and some people do so wish—pursue spiritual individualism to its limits. You can think grimly in terms of '*my* Enlightenment', disregarding everything else, and get quite a long way. Then, when you have attained your own 'individual Enlightenment' and are, as it were, resting on it, as if upon a celestial pinnacle, you can lift up your eyes to the even loftier peak of unsurpassed, perfect Enlightenment. This can be done, but there is a danger that you may get stuck, perhaps stuck indefinitely, in spiritual individualism. Even at this very high level you can end up in a sort of spiritual cul-de-sac.

It is better, therefore, if conversion in the sense of the arising of the bodhicitta occurs early on in one's spiritual life in the form of a decisive experience. It is not enough just to practise transference of merits with regard to one's everyday spiritual life and practice. One aims to precipitate the arising of the Will to Enlightenment right from the start of one's spiritual career, without settling down, even for a short period, in the path of spiritual individualism. The question is, as usual, how to do it. To understand this, we need to look at the conditions on the basis of which the bodhicitta arises.

The Will to Enlightenment is said to arise as a result of the coalescence of two trends of experience which are generally considered to be contradictory, since in ordinary experience they cannot both be pursued simultaneously. We might call these the trend of withdrawal from the world and the trend of involvement in the world.

The first of these trends represents renunciation in the extreme sense, a withdrawal from worldly activities, worldly thoughts, and secular associations. This withdrawal is aided by a particular practice, that of reflection on the faults or imperfections of conditioned existence. You reflect that life in this world, whirling round and round in the Wheel of Life, is profoundly unsatisfactory, involving as it does all sorts of disagreeable experiences. You experience physical pain and discomfort, you don't get what you want, you're separated from people you like, you have to do things you don't want to do. There's the whole wretched business of having to earn a living, doing your daily chores, taking care of your body—feeding it, clothing it, housing it, looking after it when it gets sick—not to mention taking responsibility for looking after your dependants. It all seems too much. All you want to do is get away from it all, away from the fluctuations, vicissitudes, and distractions of mundane life into the peace of the perfection of the Unconditioned, the unchanging rest of nirvāṇa.

The second trend in our experience—involvement—represents concern for living beings. You reflect: 'Well, it would be all right for me to opt out and withdraw from it all—I'd like that—but what about other people? What will happen to *them*? There are people who have a much harder time in this world than I do, who can stand it even less than I can. How will they ever get free if I abandon them?' This trend of involvement is aided by the practice of reflection on the sufferings of sentient beings. In the trend of withdrawal, you reflect on the sufferings and imperfections of conditioned existence only in so far as they affect you, but here you reflect on them as they affect other living beings. You just look around at all the people you know, your friends and acquaintances, all the people you meet, and you reflect on all their troubles and difficulties. Perhaps one or two have lost their jobs, another's marriage has broken up, yet another may have had a nervous breakdown, and there may well be someone who has recently been bereaved. If you think it over, there is not a single person you know who is not suffering in some way. Even if they seem comparatively happy in the ordinary sense, there are still things that they have to bear: separation or illness, the weakness and tiredness of old age, and finally death, which they almost certainly don't want.

Then, when you cast your gaze further afield, there is so much suffering in so many parts of the world: wars, catastrophes of various kinds, floods and famines, people dying in horrible ways. You can even think of animals and how they suffer, not only at the teeth and claws of other animals but at the hands of human beings. The whole world of living beings is involved in suffering. And when you reflect on this, you ask yourself: 'How can I possibly think simply in terms of getting out of it all on my own? How can I possibly think of getting away by myself to some private nirvāṇa, some private spiritual experience, which may be very satisfactory to me but is of no help to others?'

So there is a conflict, if you are big enough and rich enough in your nature to embrace the possibilities of such a conflict. On one hand you want to get out; on the other you want to stay here. Of course, the easy solution is simply to choose between them. There are some people who withdraw into spiritual individualism, private spiritual experience, while others remain in the world without much of a spiritual outlook at all. But although these trends are contradictory, both of them must be developed in the course of the spiritual life. The trend of withdrawal may be said to embody the wisdom aspect of the spiritual life, while the trend of involvement embodies the compassion aspect.

These two practices—reflecting on the faults of conditioned existence and reflecting on the sufferings of sentient beings—form part of a traditional method of creating the conditions in dependence upon which the bodhicitta can arise. This is the method taught by a great Indian master of the Mahāyāna, Vasubandhu, who lived, so the Mahāyāna tradition says, in the latter half of the fifth century CE. Vasubandhu enumerated four practices which would provide a basis for the arising of the bodhicitta; they are known as Vasubandhu's Four Factors. We have already identified two of these factors. The other two are 'the recollection of the Buddhas' and 'the contemplation of the virtues of the Tathāgatas' (Tathāgata being another word for Buddha).

In recollecting the Buddhas, one brings to mind the historical Buddha Śākyamuni, who lived in India about two-thousand-five-hundred years ago, and the lineage of his great predecessors of which the Buddhist tradition speaks. In particular, one reflects that these Buddhas started their spiritual careers as human beings, with their weaknesses and limitations, just as we do. Just as they managed to transcend all limitations to become Enlightened, so can we, if only we make the effort.

There are several ways of approaching the fourth practice, the contemplation of the virtues of the Tathāgatas. One can dwell on the life of an Enlightened One—the spiritual biography of the Buddha or Milarepa, for example. One can perform pujas in front of a shrine, or perhaps just sit and look at a Buddha image, really trying to get a feeling for what the image represents. Then again, one can do a visualization practice in which—to be very brief indeed—one conjures up a vivid mental picture of a particular Buddha or Bodhisattva, an embodiment of an aspect of Enlightenment such as wisdom, compassion, energy, or purity.

We can think of these Four Factors as forming a kind of sequence. First, through recollecting the Buddhas, we become convinced that Enlightenment is possible for us. Then, on seeing the faults of conditioned existence, we become detached from it, and the trend of our being is set in the direction of the Unconditioned. Thirdly, through observing the suffering of sentient beings —whether in imagination or close at hand—compassion arises, and we want to rescue not only ourselves but other beings from suffering. Then, as we contemplate the virtues of the Tathāgatas, we gradually become assimilated to them, and approach Enlightenment itself.

However, although we can think of the Four Factors sequentially in this way, the bodhicitta in fact arises in dependence on all four simultaneously. This means—returning to the tension between withdrawal and involvement—that we must not allow the tension between these two trends to relax. If we do that, we are lost. Even though they are contradictory, we have to follow both trends simultaneously, seeing the faults of conditioned existence and at the same time feeling the sufferings of sentient beings, developing both wisdom and compassion. As we develop and pursue both of these, the tension—and this tension is not psychological but spiritual—builds up and up until we simply can't go any further.

At that point, something happens. It is very difficult to describe exactly what does happen, but we can think of it provisionally as an explosion. The tension which has been generated through following simultaneously these two contradictory trends results in a breakthrough into a higher dimension of spiritual consciousness. Withdrawal and involvement are no longer two separate trends, not because they have been artificially amalgamated into one, but because the plane or level on which their duality existed, or on which it was possible for them to be two things, has been transcended. When that explosion occurs, one has the experience of being simultaneously withdrawn and involved, simultaneously out of the world and in the world. Wisdom and compassion become non-dual, not separate, not-two—without, at the same time, being simply numerically one. When this breakthrough occurs, when for the first time one is both withdrawn and involved, when wisdom and compassion are not two things side by side but one thing, then the bodhicitta has arisen. There has occurred a conversion from spiritual individualism to a life of complete selflessness—or at least such a life has been initiated.

According to the Mahāyāna, when that happens one gives expression to the experience which one has gained, to the new dimension of spiritual consciousness into which one has broken through, by taking four great vows, the Vows of the Bodhisattva:

> *However innumerable beings are, I vow to save them;*
> *However inexhaustible the passions are,*
> *I vow to extinguish them;*
> *However immeasurable the Dharmas are, I vow to master them;*
> *However incomparable the Buddha-truth is, I vow to attain it.*

So the Bodhisattva vows in the first place to deliver all beings from difficulties, both spiritual and mundane. The second vow is to destroy all spiritual defilements within one's own mind, and—through one's advice—in the minds of other living beings. The third vow is to learn the Dharma, to practise and realize it in all its aspects, and to communicate it to others. And the fourth and final vow is that in all possible ways one will help to lead all beings in the direction of Buddhahood, that is, towards unsurpassed perfect Enlightenment. When these Four Vows of the Bodhisattva are made, then one's conversion, in the sense of the arising of the will to Enlightenment, is complete.

Chapter Four

THE TURNING ABOUT
IN THE DEEPEST SEAT OF CONSCIOUSNESS

So FAR WE HAVE CERTAINLY THOUGHT of conversion in Buddhism in very radical terms. It is not enough to convert *to* Buddhism; we need to experience conversion within the context of our Buddhist practice, at ever deeper levels. It is not enough to think in terms of our own spiritual development; we need to think in terms of the spiritual welfare of all living beings. And we can think of conversion in more radical terms still. We can think of it in terms of a shift in the very nature of our experience of the world.

The ordinary experience which we have almost all the time is firmly and securely based on subject–object dualism. All our knowledge, all our thinking, takes place within the framework of this dualism—subject and object, me and you, 'me in here' and 'the world out there'. But the Enlightened mind is completely free of such dualism. It's an experience of just One Mind—*citta-mātra*, 'mind only' to use the terminology of the Yogācāra, one of the two main schools of Mahāyāna Buddhism in medieval India. The experience of the one mind is like a great expanse of water, absolutely pure, absolutely transparent, with nothing in it, not a single speck, other than the water itself.

Between the experience of One Mind and our ordinary, everyday consciousness, based as it is on subject–object dualism, there is obviously a great gulf. To go from one to the other requires a tremendous change, a complete and absolute reversal of all our usual attitudes. The Yogācāra insists on this very strongly. The spiritual life doesn't consist in a little chipping away here, a little chipping away there, a slight improvement here, a slight improvement there. It involves a complete turning about, even a complete turning upside-down. Before we can make the leap from ordinary mind, empirical mind, to the One Mind, all our established values and attitudes and ways of looking at things have to be turned topsy-turvy.

This reversal, this great change, this great death and rebirth, is what the Yogācāra terms the *parāvṛitti*, and this technical term gives us an entirely different angle on the meaning of conversion in Buddhism from those we have so far examined. Some scholars translate *parāvṛitti* as 'revulsion', but this is not really satisfactory because it implies a psychological process rather than a spiritual and metaphysical one. It is much better to use the literal translation of *parāvṛitti*—'turning about'.

The *parāvṛitti*, the turning about, is synonymous with conversion in the very deepest and most radical sense of the term. It is the central theme of the *Laṅkāvatāra Sūtra*, and indeed we may say that it is the central theme, the central concern, of the spiritual life itself. If the spiritual life doesn't turn you upside-down, if you don't feel as though you're hanging head downwards in a void, then it isn't the spiritual life. If you feel all safe and secure and firm and nicely going ahead, step by step, you haven't yet begun to live the spiritual life in earnest.

Before going into the nature of this turning about, let's have a brief look at its scriptural source, the *Laṅkāvatāra Sūtra*. In Nepal, continuing an originally Indian tradition, they have a list of ten canonical scriptures which they regard as constituting the fundamental Mahāyāna canon, and the *Laṅkāvatāra* is one of them, so we can say that it is one of the ten most important *sutras* in the Mahāyāna tradition. In fact, it was not only the Nepalis who had a high regard for this particular sūtra. It was a seminal work for the Yogācāra, and it was also central to the development of Ch'an (or Zen), having been taken from India to China (so it is said) by Bodhidharma, the founder of Ch'an Buddhism. According to the legends, Bodhidharma went wafting over the ocean from India to China on a reed, and didn't take anything with him but his robe, his bowl,—and a palm-leaf copy of the *Laṅkāvatāra Sūtra*. It was no doubt by reason of its tremendous emphasis on personal experience and inner realization that the sūtra exerted such a strong influence on Zen. Indeed, whole schools of Buddhism have devoted themselves to the study of just this one text; it is certainly one of the most exhaustive and profound sūtras in the Buddhist canon.

The full title of the work is the *Saddharma-laṅkāvatāra Sūtra*. *Sūtra* means a discourse of the Buddha, *saddharma* means 'the good law', or 'the real truth', and *laṅkavatāra* means 'entry into Laṅkā', so we can render the whole title as 'The Buddha's discourse on the entry of the real truth into Laṅkā'. Laṅkā is a city or castle situated on a mountain-top in the ocean somewhere off the Indian coast. In Indian literature, of course, Laṅkā usually stands for what we call Sri Lanka, but here no such specific identification can be inferred; in this sūtra we are in the realm of myth rather than geography.

The sūtra is a fairly lengthy work of nine chapters, the English translation by D.T. Suzuki running to about 300 pages.* It contains a large number of extremely profound and valuable teachings, though in a rather scattered form, the text being an anthology of extracts or excerpts in no systematic order. But of

---

* *The Lankavatara Sutra*, trans. D.T. Suzuki, Routledge, London 1932.

the immense number of topics with which the sūtra deals, we are here concerned with only one: the *parāvṛitti*, the turning about.

The first chapter of the *Laṅkāvatāra* is called 'The Invitation of Rāvaṇa', Rāvaṇa being the king of the Rākshasas, the beings who inhabit the island of Laṅkā. In Buddhist texts Rāvaṇa appears as a wise sage, a great disciple of the Buddha, but it is interesting to note that in Hindu texts such as the *Rāmāyaṇa* he is the villain of the piece; this only goes to show that there is always more than one way of looking at not only a particular religious doctrine but even a particular individual. According to the introduction to the sūtra, Rāvaṇa invites the Buddha to preach (a conventional Buddhist procedure—one is generally invited to preach rather than taking the initiative oneself). In response the Buddha delivers a succinct and profound discourse, as a result of which Rāvaṇa experiences the *parāvṛitti*.

It seems to him that the whole universe vanishes and all that is left is an expanse of absolute consciousness, or absolute mind, within which there is no differentiation of subject and object. Furthermore, he hears a voice proclaiming that this is the state which has to be realized. It is this experience, this change in Rāvaṇa's consciousness from awareness of the ordinary external universe in all its discreteness and diversity to awareness of absolute mind, free from all distinction between universe and void, which constitutes what is called the *parāvṛitti*.

To understand how this process of turning about happens, we need to refer to a rather technical but absolutely fundamental aspect of the Yogācāra teaching called the system of the eight *vijñānas*. *Vijñāna* is usually translated as 'consciousness', but that is not exactly accurate. The prefix *vi-* means 'to divide' or 'to discriminate', and *jñāna* means 'knowledge' or 'awareness', so we can translate *vijñāna* as 'discriminating awareness'. *Vijñāna* therefore refers to awareness of an object not just in a pure mirror-like way but in a way which discriminates the object as being of a particular type and belonging to a particular class, species, or whatever. In the Yogācāra teaching there are eight of these *vijñānas*, eight forms of discriminating awareness or consciousness. The first five are the five 'sense *vijñānas*', the modes of discriminating awareness which operate through the five senses—through the eye with respect to form, the ear with respect to sound, and so on.

The sixth consciousness is called the *mano-vijñāna*. *Mano* means simply 'mind', so this is discriminating awareness functioning through mind. Mind, by the way, is usually classified in Buddhism as a sort of sixth sense, so it doesn't have a special elevated position above the five sense consciousnesses. According to Yogācāra psychology, there are two aspects of *mano-vijñāna*. The first of these is awareness of what we might describe as 'ideas of sense'—in other words, the mind's awareness of impressions presented to it by the five senses. And the second aspect is awareness of ideas which arise independently of sense-perception, out of the mind itself. This latter aspect of *mano-vijñāna* is of three kinds. First of all, there are the ideas and impressions which arise in the course of meditation, as when one experiences light which doesn't have its origin in any sense impression but comes from the mind itself. Then secondly there are functions such as imagination, comparison, and reflection. And thirdly there are the images perceived in dreams, which again come not from sense impressions but directly from the mind itself. All this is the *mano-vijñāna*.

Seventhly, there is the *klishto-mano-vijñāna*. *Klishto* means 'afflicted', or 'suffering', and it also means 'defiled', because defilement is a source of suffering. This mode of awareness, therefore, is afflicted or defiled by a dualistic outlook. Whatever it experiences, it interprets dualistically in terms of a subject and an object—subject as self, and object as world or universe. So everything is seen in terms of pairs of opposites: good and bad, true and false, right and wrong, existence and non-existence, and so on. This dualistic mode of discriminative awareness or consciousness is, of course, what characterizes the way we usually live and work.

The eighth consciousness is called the *ālaya-vijñāna*. Strictly speaking, however, this is not a *vijñāna* at all, because in it there is no discrimination, but just awareness. *Ālaya* literally means a repository or store, or even treasury; we are all familiar with the word in the compound 'Himālaya', which means 'the abode of snow' or 'the repository of snow'. This 'store consciousness' has two aspects: the 'relative *ālaya*' and the 'absolute *ālaya*'. The relative *ālaya* consists of, or contains, the impressions left deep in the mind by all our previous experiences. Whatever we have done or said or thought or experienced, a trace or residue of it remains there; nothing is absolutely lost. The relative *ālaya*, in fact, is not unlike Jung's collective unconscious, although this is a very approximate analogy which cannot be pushed too far. The Yogācārin School conceives of the impressions which are deposited in the *ālaya-vijñāna*, the consequences of our various thoughts and deeds, as 'seeds' (*bījas*). In other words, these impressions are not passive; they are not just like the impression left by a seal in a piece of wax. They are *active* impressions, left like seeds in the soil, and when conditions are favourable they sprout up and produce fruits.

Ālaya in its absolute aspect is Reality itself, conceived of in terms of pure awareness free from all trace of subjectivity and objectivity. It is a pure, continuous, and non-dimensional—or even multi-dimensional—awareness in which there is nothing of which anyone is aware, nor anyone who is aware. It is awareness without subject and without object, something which is very difficult for us to apprehend.

It is at the level of the *ālaya*—the 'deepest seat of consciousness' as Suzuki calls it*—that the turning about with which we are concerned takes place. We can say (although the *Laṅkāvatāra* itself does not actually say this explicitly) that the turning about takes place at the borderline separating the relative *ālaya* (that is, *ālaya* as a sort of collective unconscious) from the *ālaya* as Reality, as pure awareness.

How this actually takes place is not at all easy to describe, but the texts give us some hints. What we can say is that as we go through our lives, we have all sorts of experiences of one kind or another, all the time, every day, every hour, every minute; and as a result more and more impressions accumulate in the relative *ālaya*. These impressions are known as 'impure seeds', because the thoughts, words, and deeds which deposited or sowed them are defiled by our dualistic outlook, especially—to put it in more ethico-psychological terms—by our craving, our aversion, and our fundamental spiritual ignorance. However, just as, in consequence of our ordinary actions, we can deposit impure seeds, so we can also deposit and accumulate 'pure seeds'. These are pure impressions or traces, produced by our more spiritual thoughts, words, and deeds. The more we devote ourselves to the spiritual life, the more we accumulate spiritual impressions or traces—or pure seeds—in the relative *ālaya*.

There comes a point when so many of these pure seeds are amassed in the relative *ālaya* that the absolute *ālaya* (which 'borders' on the relative *ālaya*) starts to push on them. And as the absolute *ālaya* presses on the pure seeds, they in turn bring their weight to bear upon the impure seeds, and in the end they push them right out. It is this pushing out of the impure seeds that constitutes the turning about within the *ālaya*, within the deepest

* D.T. Suzuki, *Manual of Zen Buddhism*, Grove Press, New York 1960, p.14.

seat of consciousness. Once this has taken place, a complete transformation is set up within the entire *vijñāna* system, and the eight *vijñānas* are transformed into what are called the five *jñānas*, usually translated as the five knowledges or wisdoms. The eight modes of discriminating awareness are transformed into five modes of pure—that is, non-discriminating—awareness or wisdom. Hence the term *jñāna. Vijñāna* means discriminating awareness, but *jñāna* means simply awareness.

These five *jñānas* or wisdoms represent the five aspects of Enlightenment, and they are personified in Buddhist iconography as five Buddhas of various colours. The first five *vijñānas*, the sense-consciousnesses, are collectively transformed into what is called the All-performing Wisdom. This wisdom, which is capable of doing anything, is personified by the green Buddha, Amoghasiddhi, whose name means 'Infallible Success'. So the five ordinary sense consciousnesses start functioning as the all-performing wisdom, or the all-performing awareness. The next one, the *mano-vijñāna*, the mind consciousness, is transformed into Distinguishing Wisdom, the wisdom which appreciates the infinite variety of existence down to even the minutest differences. This is personified by the red Buddha, Amitābha—'Infinite Light'.

As for the *klishṭo-mano-vijñāna*, the defiled mind consciousness, this is transformed into the Wisdom of Equality. It is a characteristic of the defiled mind consciousness to see things in terms of subject–object duality, in terms of opposition or conflict, but once the turning about has taken place, this is transformed into an awareness which sees everything as equal, sees everything with complete objectivity, and has the same attitude of compassion towards all. It is not that differences are obliterated, but one becomes aware that running through the differences—and even not different from the differences—is a thread of unity, of sameness. All things are equally void, equally one pure mind.

This is personified by the yellow Buddha, Ratnasambhava, whose name means 'Jewel-born One'.

The relative *ālaya* is transformed into what is called the Mirror-like Wisdom, which reflects everything impartially and without distortion, which does not stick or cling to anything, but sees things just as they are. This wisdom is personified by the dark blue Buddha, Akshobhya, 'the Imperturbable'.

The absolute *ālaya*, of course, is not transformed at all, because it does not need to be transformed. It is equivalent to the fifth wisdom, the Wisdom of the Dharmadhātu, the wisdom of the universe perceived as fully pervaded by Reality, the Absolute Wisdom. This is personified by the white Buddha, Vairocana, whose name means 'the Illuminator'. Just as white is composed of all the colours of the rainbow, so this is the basic wisdom of which the other four are aspects.*

In this way, after the turning about at the *ālaya* level has taken place, the eight consciousnesses become the five wisdoms, and one is utterly transformed—transformed into an Enlightened being, a Buddha, functioning in these five different ways, with these five modes of awareness. In other words, as a result of the *parāvṛitti*, as a result of this turning about, this conversion, one's whole being and one's whole consciousness is transformed, translated, from an unenlightened level to an Enlightened level.

There still remains unanswered, of course, the usual practical question. How do we bring about the *parāvṛitti*? It can hardly come about by accident. According to the Yogācāra, although we have eight modes of consciousness, we normally function only on the basis of the first seven. Our five sense-consciousnesses function vigorously all the time we are awake, the mind

---

* For more details of the iconography and symbolism of the Five Buddhas, see Vessantara, *Meeting the Buddhas*, Windhorse, Glasgow 1993, Part 2.

consciousness keeps on functioning whether we are awake or asleep, and the defiled mind consciousness is of course very active indeed. But the *ālaya*—the relative *ālaya* and especially the absolute *ālaya*—is normally hidden from us. The highest level of consciousness to which we normally have access is the *klishṭo-mano-vijñāna*, the level of the mind defiled by duality, by seeing things in terms of opposites, especially subject and object, self and other. So this is the level on which we have to operate. We have to work with the tools that lie to hand.

It is at this level, therefore, with this dualistic outlook, that we take up various spiritual practices. For instance, when we take up meditation our ultimate goal is non-dualistic, but our practice is necessarily dualistic. Here we are sitting meditating, while the object of our meditation—our breathing, or maybe a mantra—is, as it were, over there. The basis is dualistic because that is how we are constituted, that is the level on which we are functioning. All our various religious practices and spiritual exercises, especially meditation, are taken up on the level of the defiled mind consciousness. But by means of these practices on that level, impressions of a better type are left; pure seeds, as the Yogācārins call them, are accumulated. And eventually, as we practise day by day, week by week, year by year, enough pure seeds are deposited in the relative *ālaya* for the turning about to take place.

We should not feel discouraged at the thought of all the time and effort this will take. It's rather like dropping a depth charge. If you are out at sea in a boat and you want to cause an explosion right down in the depths, you may have to spend hours or even days assembling the various component parts of the depth charge, and priming and adjusting the mechanism. And you do all that on the deck, even though you want to produce an effect many fathoms below. It's no use getting impatient and thinking: 'Why waste all this time putting it all together here on deck? Why not just throw the stuff overboard and hope for the best?' Spiritual practice is rather like that. It is easy to get discouraged, and think: 'I've been meditating (or doing some other practice) for all these weeks and months and years, but I'm still not Enlightened. I haven't even entered the Stream. What's going on?' Even when we feel we're not getting anywhere, though, the important thing is to carry on, because all this work has to be done at the level of the defiled mind consciousness in order to produce the required result at the level of the *ālaya*.

This reminds me of a story I heard when I was in southern India many years ago, visiting the ashram of Ramaṇa Maharshi, one of the most famous Hindu teachers of this century. Someone had apparently asked him how it is that our spiritual practice sometimes seems to have so little effect. We do all this meditation, we read all these scriptures, we give all these gifts, but nothing seems to happen. We're just the same, apparently. So the questioner wanted to know why this was—why was there no change, no improvement? In reply, Ramaṇa Maharshi told a little story.

He said: 'Once upon a time there was a man who wanted to split into two an enormous rock. So he went up to the rock with a great sledge-hammer, and swinging it with all his might he delivered a terrific blow, right in the centre of the rock. Nothing happened. So he drew a deep breath, flexed his muscles, and delivered another great blow in the same spot. Nothing happened. The rock stayed perfectly intact, just as it had been before. So, in the same way, sweating more and more, struggling more and more, panting for breath, the man delivered blow after blow, until he had struck the rock nineteen times. Still nothing happened. There was not a mark, not a dent. The man thought, "All right, now or never," collected all his strength, and gave one last tremendous blow. And with that twentieth blow, the rock split neatly, cleanly, quietly, into two halves.'

So were the first nineteen blows completely useless? Was it just that last one that did the trick? No. Although no result could be seen, with each blow the rock was weakened along the line where the hammer struck. The twentieth blow just gave the last touch which was needed to split the rock. Though the results could not be seen, they were there all the time.

It is just like that when we work at the level of the defiled mind consciousness, hammering away at the rock of the empirical self. It may seem that our spiritual practices aren't producing any results. We may think: 'I'm the same person that I always was. I get angry just as easily. I'm just as greedy, just as interested in worldly things. Nothing has happened.' But all the time, at a deeper level, something *is* happening: blows are being struck, pure seeds are accumulating, the depth charge is being prepared. The important thing is to keep going, not to get discouraged by apparent failures or temporary setbacks, not to give up.

There are just two more crucial points to be stressed. The teaching of *parāvṛitti* draws attention to the fact that in the religious life an intellectual understanding is not enough. People who have read many books on the subject might think they have a good understanding of Buddhism, but according to the *Laṅkā vatāra* this is not enough. 'No dependence on words and letters' is the Zen way of putting it.* Through its doctrine of *parāvṛitti*, the *Laṅkāvatāra* is saying that there must also be a definite spiritual experience. There must be a conversion, a tremendous change in our mode of awareness, our way of looking at things, and our way of behaving, for there to be any real spiritual life at all. This is the first basic point that this doctrine is making. Most of the time we are just acquiring intellectual information from external sources; there is no fundamental modification of the quality of consciousness itself. But it is this radical transformation in the mode of our consciousness—as the Buddha says in the *Laṅkāvatāra*—which is the point of the whole exercise. There

---

* See Sangharakshita, *The Essence of Zen*, Windhorse, Glasgow 1992.

must be this turning about, even turning upside-down—or, as Nietzsche says, 'a transvaluation of all values'—in which we see things not just in a slightly different way, but in a totally different way, with all our previous values reversed. We must be prepared even for that.

The other significant point implied by this doctrine is that the turning about, this conversion, is sudden—that it takes place in an instant. Here we can see at once the connection with the Zen idea of 'sudden Enlightenment', and it should now be clear what is really meant by this idea. Unfortunately it is still commonly taken to mean that you can get Enlightened easily and quickly, without any trouble at all. You just go along to the library, take out one or two books on Zen, read them, and hey presto! There you are!—Conveniently forgetting that the books themselves say 'No dependence on words and letters'. Indeed, 'a book on Zen' is really an absolute contradiction in terms. Where there are books, there is no Zen—or one might say, where there is Zen, there are no books. At least, there is in Zen no dependence on books, no reliance upon them. Conversion, Enlightenment, or *satori*, is sudden only in the sense that the splitting of the rock is sudden. All the other nineteen blows had to be made. In truth, then, the splitting is not sudden at all. It only appears to be so because its coming about has been taking place at a different, deeper level, hidden from view.

So it is true that the *parāvṛitti*, the conversion, is sudden, that it takes place in the twinkling of an eye, but the preparation for it takes a very long time. There are no short cuts; a very great deal of discipline, training, and meditation is necessary. This is true not only with regard to Zen, not only with regard to the Yogācāra School or the teaching of the *Laṅkāvatāra*. It holds good for all forms of Buddhism. Whether you take up the Theravāda, or Zen, or Tibetan Buddhism, the culminating experience may come suddenly in a flash, but the process of building up to that experience takes a very long time. It may take the whole of your life. But if you believe that the experience itself is worthwhile—is indeed the only truly meaningful aim of human life—then of course you will not begrudge the time spent.

In this overview of the meaning of conversion in Buddhism, I hope that we have clearly established at least one fact. This is that conversion in Buddhism is a complex and arduous task. It is all too easy to say *Buddhaṁ saraṇaṁ gacchāmi* and consider oneself to be converted to Buddhism, but it is really not so simple. Conversion to Buddhism or conversion within Buddhism, whether in terms of Going for Refuge, Stream Entry, the arising of the will to Enlightenment, or the turning about of the mind in the deepest seat of consciousness, is by no means easy. We have to build up to it over a period of days, weeks, months, and even years, because it takes place on a very high level indeed, a level on which we do not usually function.

This is, however, the level on which we have to function eventually if we take our Buddhism seriously, if it is to mean more to us than an intellectual pastime—if, in short, we are really to experience conversion. And our conversion is complete only when the aim of the Buddhist path is fulfilled, when our practice of Buddhism has taken us through these levels of conversion right to the turning about in the deepest seat of consciousness, to Enlightenment itself.

Index